Progressive Hymns

Edited by Megan M. Rohrer

© 2020 Wilgefortis

PROGRESSIVE HYMNS
Edited by Megan Rohrer

Cover design by Megan Rohrer.

All rights reserved under International and Pan-American Copyright Conventions. Published in the United States by Wilgefortis.

Except for use in worship, choir practice and performances, brief quotations in critical articles, reviews, no part of this book may be reproduced in any form without the permission of the author.

ISBN: 978-0-359-94056-1

For the members and friends of Grace Lutheran in San Francisco.

Join us in person (Sundays at 10:30 am) or online via Facebook live on the Rev. Dr. Megan Rohrer's Facebook page.

www.gracesf.com

Other Books by Megan Rohrer

Other Books in the Travel Faithfully Series:
Prayers from Philadelphia: Life, Liberty and the Pursuit of Happiness
Prayers from the Caribbean: Injury, Struggle and Liberation
Sacred Waters: How to Accept Blessings When They Find You
Prayers from Norway: Untangling Our Shame of Body, Mind and Politics
Prayers from Ireland: Light Dawns in a Weary World
New Wonders: Lessons Learned at the End of a Long Winding Road

Other Faithful Books for Adults:
The Chaplain's Heart: An Embodied Guide to Ministry of Presence
Bible Stories: Reimagining Between the Lines
With a Day Like Yours Couldn't You Use a Little Grace
Queerly Lutheran

LGBTQ Anthologies
Vanguard Revisited: The Queer Faith, Sex & Politics of The Youth of San Francisco's Tenderloin (ed. with Joey Plaster)
Manifest: Transitional Wisdom on Male Privilege (ed. with Zander Keig)
Letters for My Brothers: Transitional Wisdom in Retrospect (ed. with Zander Keig)

Good News Children's Book Series

The Radical Jesus Story	Too Sick for Church
The Fabulous Creation Story	Never Again
Jesus' Family	The Parable of the Succulent
Church Bugs	The Children's Crumbs
Boy, Girl or Both	Faithful Families
Transgender Children of God	What to Wear to Church
Mr. Grumpy Christian	

Introduction	4
Seasonal Hymns	6
ADVENT	7
Luke's Magnificats	7
Justice Wonderland	8
CHRISTMAS	9
Baby Jesus By and By	9
Justice Thou Art	10
A Fragile Infant is Our God	11
LENT	12
Were You There	12
Triduum Song	13
EASTER	14
Christ's Alive Today	14
Joy to the World, Christ is Raised	15
Joyful, Joyful Easter Morning	16
Thematic Hymns	17
JUSTICE	18
Rise Up, Children of God	18
Ain't Got Time for Incremental Justice	19
What a Friendship	20
Made the Whole World a Holy Land	21
CREATION AND RECREATION	22
Beautiful Jesus	22
We Walk in Sight of All the World	23
This is a Sacred World	24
Arising, Illumining Source all Divine	25
We Are People Transforming	26

Liturgical Hymns — 27

GATHERING SONGS — 28
- *Gathering Song to the Tune of Lady Gaga's Paparazzi* — 28
- *Call to Worship to the Tune of The Beatles' Blackbird* — 29
- *Call to Worship to the Tune of Joni Mitchell's Big Yellow Taxi* — 30
- *Gathering Song to the Tune of Bob Dylan's Times They are a Changin'* — 31

GOSPEL ACCLAMATIONS — 32
- *Gospel Acclamation to the tune of Lady Gaga's Poker Face* — 32
- *Gospel Acclamation to the tune of The Beatles' Yellow Submarine* — 33
- *Gospel Acclamation to the tune of Joni Mitchell's Twisted* — 33

PRAYERS OF THE PEOPLE — 34
- *Prayers of the People to the Tune of The Beatles' Across the Universe* — 34
- *Prayers of the People to the Tune of Lady Gaga's Bad Romance* — 35
- *Prayers of the People to the Tune of Bob Dylan's To Make You Feel My Love* — 36
- *Prayers of the People to the Tune of Joni Mitchell's Clouds* — 37
- *Prayers of the People to the Tune of Stay with Me by Sam Smith* — 39
- *Prayers of the People to the Tune of the Eurythmics' Sweet Dreams (Are Made of These)* — 40

PASSING THE PEACE — 41
- *Passing of the Peace to the Tune of The Beatles' I Wanna Hold Your Hand* — 41
- *Passing of the Peace to the Tune of Joni Mitchell's The River* — 42

OFFERING — 43
- *Offering Song to the tune of Adelle's Rolling in the Deep* — 43

COMMUNION — 45
- *Communion to the Tune of The Beatles' Hey Jude* — 45
- *Communion to the Tune of Jodi Mitchell's All I Want* — 46
- *Communion to the Tune of Lady Gaga's Telephone* — 47
- *Communion to the tune of The House of the Rising Sun* — 49
- *Communion to the Tune of Cups as Performed by Anna Kendrick* — 50

SENDING SONGS	51
Go in Peace to the Tune of The Beatles' Let it Be	*51*
Sending to the Tune of Lady Gaga's Just Dance	*52*
Sending to the Tune of Joni Mitchell's Circle Game	*53*
Go My Children, With My Blessing	*54*
God Be with You Through Transition	*55*
Blessing and Dismissal	*56*
Go in Peace to the Tune of A-Ha's Take on Me	*56*
About the Authors	**57**

Introduction

Both Martin Luther and Sister Mary Clarence, of Sister Act, paired standard hymns with contemporary tunes. Like them, I work mightily to link the Good News to words and artistic expressions that speak contemporary communities. Faith leaders, congregations and denominations have also taken on this work in an effort to evaluate the ways we have fueled systems of injustice.

During this time of sheltering in place, due to the coronavirus, it feels more important than ever to share creative worship resources. faith. When fear, stress and trauma make it difficult focus and gather in groups, we are particularly in need of liberating lyrics.

I sincerely hope the hymns in this collection will contribute to the love, care and faith people are sharing during these trying times. I also hope to the updated lyrics to classic hymns will support decolonizing efforts taking place. Most of the hymns in this collection are lyrics that I have written over 18 years of work in Presbyterian, Episcopal and Lutheran communities. Some, like those from my Lady Gaga and Beatles Masses have received more attention than others.

A few were written by Orion, Judith Dancer, the Rev. Dr. Susan Strouse and Sharon Reinbott. Their wonderful work deserves a wider audience. I hope this publication will inspire them to continue creating additional liturgical resources.

Because the hymns collected here were written for extraordinarily diverse congregants, some may speak to you more than others. Like all faithful ventures, they are shared in hopes of sparking faith in others. I sincerely hope they inspire you. May they be as much of a gift your you and your communities as they have been to me and the communities I have been so honored to serve.

Blessings upon blessings,

The Rev. Dr. Megan Rohrer
April 18, 2020
San Francisco, CA

Seasonal Hymns

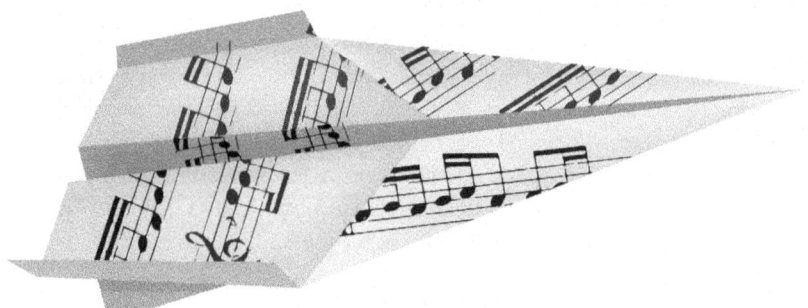

Advent

Luke's Magnificats

This hymn, set to the tune of Thy Holy Wings, amplifies the words of Elizabeth and Mary, as found in the Gospel of Luke. Verse 1 and 4 are the words of Elizabeth. Verses 2 and 3 are the words of Mary.

I'm filled by the Holy Spirit and cannot contain my cry
Blessed is she who truly believed it, the promises of the Most High
Blessed are you among women, blessed is the fruit of your womb
My child lept with joy within me, God's love is about to bloom

My soul and my spirit, magnify the Creating God
Although they call me lowly, I have stood where angels trod
Now that I carry God within me, the unjust will surly fall
Hope will find the hopeless and there will be food enough for all

My child will be a prophet and prepare our way
Bring knowledge of salvation, a dawn for this new day
Illuminate the darkness, fade the shadow of death
Teach peace to all who are warring and guide our feet out of this mess

I'm filled by the Holy Spirit and cannot contain my cry
Blessed is she who truly believed it, the promises of the Most High
Good news and great joy for all people, victory o'er the tomb
Glory to God in the highest heaven, God's love is about to bloom

Lyrics: Megan Rohrer

Justice Wonderland

This hymn, set to the tune of Winter Wonderland, asks those gathered to commit to work for justice in the upcoming year.

Sleighbells ring are you listenin'
To the voices we've been missin'
The first will be last, atone for the past
Protecting the vulnerable this year

Gone away is recession
Now we must fight oppression
We want equal pay, with a living wage
Ringing in justice this New Year

Bridge:
This year we'll put down our privilege
And lift the one's racism has held down
Justice is the true meaning of Christmas
So, spread it through the country and the towns

Strong in faith we won't cower
When we speak truth to power
It's time to reform, decolonize the norm
God's work our hands this New Year

Lyrics: Megan Rohrer

Christmas

Baby Jesus By and By

This hymn, set to the tune of Sweet By and By, includes portions of the Nicene Creed and is also appropriate for Epiphany.

There's a mother that's fairer than the day
Magnified to bring forth God's holy name
Mary gave birth to Jesus in the hay
And the Earth would never be the same

<u>Chorus:</u>
Born this day in a barn
Unto us a Savior is born
Born this day in a barn
Unto us a Savior is born

An angel woke the shepherds that night
And told them to follow a star
In the deep darkness shown a great light
Calling astrologers from afar   *Chorus*

Christ Jesus in a manger He lay
God of God begotten not made
He suffered, died and rose on the third day
In the glory our debts He has paid   *Chorus*

Lyrics: Megan Rohrer

Justice Thou Art

This hymn, set to the tune of How Great Thou Art, is appropriate for both Christmas and Epiphany.

The birth of God, in a lowly manger
Brings hope to all who live in poverty
Born in Palestine amid fear and anger
Fled to Egypt as a refugee

Chorus
Then from her[1] soul, Mary starts to sing
Pondering in her heart, justice thou art
Then from her soul, Mary starts to sing
Pondering in her heart, justice thou art

Faithful astrologers, from distant nations
Greet the babe, with incense, gold and myrrh
The bright north star, lights Christ's ordination
The great Rabbi, not even death can detour
Chorus

Be born this day, a peaceful reformation
And my life, be God's hands and feet
Ever in my heart, a constant revelation
That I will share, when I meet Christ on the street
Chorus

Lyrics: Megan Rohrer

---

[1] If repeating the chorus at the end, replace word "her" with "your."

A Fragile Infant is Our God

This hymn, set to the tune of A Mighty Fortress, helps us understand the peculiarity of God choosing to become embodied as a fragile child.

A fragile infant is our God
Flesh and bone that's wailing
The King of Kings dependent on mom
And the diapers He is wearing
He was born in Palestine
During the census time
Mary rode an ass
So, they could pay their tax
The light of lights Christ Jesus

A simple God born near the cows
Will live a life of humility
Teaching us to love in the here and now
And never fear vulnerability
He'll die so we may live
Forgives so we may forgive
In baptism we are named
Ending the need for shame
Saved by grace, through faith forever

A fragile infant is our God
Flesh and bone that's wailing
The King of Kings dependent on mom
And the diapers He is wearing
He was born in Palestine
During the census time
Mary rode an ass
So, they could pay their tax
The light of lights Christ Jesus
Celebrate the birth of Jesus

Lyrics: Megan Rohrer

Lent

Were You There

This hymn, set to the tune of Were You There, speaks to some of the deep injustices of our world. You can add the verse "were you there when they crucified my Lord" at the beginning and end of the song.

Were you there when they walked the Trail of Tears
Were you there when they walked the Trail of Tears
Oh, sometimes it causes me to tremble, tremble, tremble
Were you there when they walked the Trail of Tears

Were you there when they were forced into slavery
Were you there when they were forced into slavery
Oh, sometimes it causes me to tremble, tremble, tremble
Were you there when they were forced into slavery

Were you there when they put them in the stoves
Were you there when they put them in the stoves
Oh, sometimes it causes me to tremble, tremble, tremble
Were you there when they put them in the stoves

Were you there when they locked them in the cage
Were you there when they locked them in the cage
Oh, sometimes it causes me to tremble, tremble, tremble
Were you there when they locked them in the cage

Lyrics: Megan Rohrer

Triduum Song

This hymn, set to the tune of This is My Song or Finlandia, chronicles Jesus' journey towards the cross as narrated in the Gospel of Mark.

Sit here and pray, O faithful generation
Take away from me, this cup of suffering
Wait here and pray, your spirit, but not your flesh is willing
Not my will but yours, O Great Mystery
Are you still sleeping, enough resting
The hour has come, for my destiny

Judas arrived, said "Rabbi" and he kissed me
A sign of love was how I was betrayed
Day after day, in the temple I was teaching
Yet with clubs and swords you arrest me this way
A certain young man wore nothing but some linen
He ran away, but the linen stayed

Now at the festival they released a prisoner
Pilate asked would it be Barabbas or me
This sealed my fate they yelled "crucify him"
Leaders of faith were blinded by jealousy
They put me in robes, whipped and scorned me
My cross was carried by Simon of Cyrene

They led me up to the place called Golgotha
On a wooden cross they nailed my fragile body
Save yourself, they all shouted at me
I cried "Eloi, Eloi, lema sabachthani"
I breathed my last and the temple curtain tore in two
From a distance, looking on were both the Mary's

Lyrics: Megan Rohrer

Easter

Christ's Alive Today

This hymn, set to the tune of Soon and Very Soon, chronicles the post-resurrection sightings of Jesus.

The women led the way, O, Christ's alive today
They were the first to say, Yes, Christ's alive today
Victory o'er the grave, O, Christ's alive today

Refrain:
Hallelujah, hallelujah, Christ's alive today

The disciples hid in fear, O, Christ's alive today
Jesus drew them near, Yes, Christ's alive today
Put your finger here, O, Christ's alive today
Refrain

They said Jesus was dead O, Christ's alive today
Couldn't recognize his head, Yes, Christ's alive today
Then Jesus broke the bread, O, Christ's alive today
Refrain

Jesus told them how to fish, O, Christ's alive today
Cooked them up a dish, Yes, Christ's alive today
Can you imagine this? O, Christ's alive today
Refrain

Each stranger that I meet, O, Christ's alive today
The homeless on the street, Yes, Christ's alive today
Through my hands and feet, O, Christ's alive today
Refrain

Lyrics: Megan Rohrer

Joy to the World, Christ is Raised

This hymn, set to the tune of Joy to the World, provides a melodic connection between Christmas and Easter. Some of the original verses of Joy to the World may be added as appropriate.

Joy to the world, Christ is raised
And love is in full bloom
Let ev'ry heart, go forth and proclaim
They found an empty tomb
They found an empty tomb
They found, they found an empty tomb

Joy to the ones, who have been shamed
The lost all are found
Forgiveness grows, hope and peace
Our lives are now unbound
Our lives are now unbound
Our lives, our lives are now unbound

Joy to the earth, Spring has sprung
And new life abounds
Flowers, trees and honeybees
Our world is Holy ground
Our world is Holy ground
Our world, our world is Holy ground

Lyrics: Megan Rohrer

Joyful, Joyful Easter Morning

This hymn, set to the tune of Joyful, Joyful We Adore Thee, musically captures the festive joy of Easter morning celebrations.

Joyful, joyful Easter morning
Empty tomb, sign of God's love
Breaking bread and faith restoring
Ascending to the throne above
End the pain of isolation
Wipe our shame and guilt away
Bring justice without hesitation
Make us a kin-dom today

All creation springs to life around you
Ever loved and ever blessed
Good News in all we say and do
Seeking to embody our best
Help us learn to love self and other
Both our friends and enemies
Saved by grace, faith rediscovered
Liberated and set free

Joyful, joyful Easter morning
Empty tomb, sign of God's love
Breaking bread and faith restoring
Ascending to the throne above
End the pain of isolation
Wipe our shame and guilt away
Bring justice without hesitation
Make us a kin-dom today

Lyrics: Megan Rohrer

Thematic Hymns

Justice

Rise Up, Children of God

This hymn, set to the tune of Rise Up, O Saints of God, helps individuals explore the implicit biases they carry and work for civil rights for all.

Rise up children of God
From all oppressions turn
Disengage from your selfish ways
Listen, repent and learn

Speak out children of God
Live lives that are Good News
Let your forgiveness know no end
As we learn from our neighbor's truth

March on children of God
Ever toward Martin's[2] dream
Amplify those with the most at stake
Till justice flows as a living stream

Commit your hearts to growth
Loving all as Jesus taught
Open your minds to needed change
Repair our deeds and thought

Rise up children of God
From all oppressions turn
Disengage from your selfish ways
Listen, repent and learn

Lyrics: Megan Rohrer

---

[2] You can also use MLK instead.

Ain't Got Time for Incremental Justice

This hymn, set to the tune of I Want Jesus to Walk With Me, speaks to the injustice in our world- including mass shootings, differing abilities, death of children, racism, the refugee crisis and immigration. The hymn, inspired by Amos 5, demands justice like an ever-flowing stream.

Another momma weeps for her baby
Too many sirens and not enough peace
Ain't got time for incremental justice
I was promised an everflowin' stream

Refugees are locked in cages
Despite the horrors they flee
Ain't got time for incremental justice
I was promised an everflowin' stream

Another night, cold and hungry
Sleepin' rough out on the street
Ain't got time for incremental justice
I was promised an everflowin' stream

Abandon privilege, make reparations
Share your wealth, abolish poverty
Ain't got time for incremental justice
I was promised an everflowin' stream

Come on Jesus, roll with me
Come on Jesus, roll with me
Ain't got time for incremental justice
I was promised an everflowin' stream

Ain't got time for incremental justice
New creation begins with me

Lyrics: Megan Rohrer

What a Friendship

This hymn, set to the tune of What a Friend we Have in Jesus, describes friendship of mutuality, shared vision and of celebrative community. It refers to Jesus' saying that he calls us friends, not servants and hopefully has the effect of toppling the hierarchy of God-Human-Animal-Plant-Mineral that pervades much of our religious thinking.

What a friendship we have chosen! Not as servants of a king,
Friends that Jesus has invited, Trust and freedom honouring.
How shall we respond in wonder? How receive in joy unfurled?
We will trust the constant presence and befriend the Friend of the World.

What a vision we're creating! All the earth restored and whole,
Freedom for the captive nations, healed in body and in soul.
Strong in trust and in compassion, May we see the joy unfurled!
One with God and one in visions, we befriend the Friend of the World.

What a fellowship we're sharing! What a kinship we've begun!
Sharing bread with good companions, celebrating work well done.
Wider we expand the circle, wider is the joy unfurled:
As we stand with all creation, we befriend the Friend of the World.

Lyrics: Sharon Reinbott

Made the Whole World a Holy Land

This hymn, set to the tune of He's Got the Whole World in His Hands and inspired by Julian of Norwich, encourages Interfaith unity, peace and climate justice.

She made the whole world a Holy Land
He made the whole wide world a Holy Land
They made the whole world a Holy Land
We made the whole world a Holy Land

She made Jews & Muslims a Holy Band
He made Sikhs & Hindus a Holy Band
They made Jains & Buddhists a Holy Band
We made the whole world a Holy Land

She made Southern Baptists a Holy Band
He made Roman Catholics a Holy Band
They even made Lutherans a Holy Band
We made the whole world a Holy Land

She made North Korea a Holy Land
He made Tanzania a Holy Land
They made Sri Lanka a Holy Land
We made the whole world a Holy Land

She made birds and mammals a Holy Band
He made fish and humans a Holy Band
All creation's a Holy Band
We made the whole word a Holy Land

Lyrics: Orion

Creation and Recreation

Beautiful Jesus

This hymn, set to the tune of Beautiful Savior, encourages whole body care, body positivity justice, diversity and compassion.

Beautiful Jesus, eighth day of creation
Living stream of hope and life.
Bringer of justice, embodied liberation
You make creation new again.

All that's within me, all that I carry
Child of God, and wholesome be
God's new creation, baptized beloved,
Fiercely and wonderfully made.

Gathered and present, with, in and through us
Growing in faith, we all sing
God's new creation, baptized beloved,
Fiercely and wonderfully made.

To all our neighbors, beyond our understanding,
Gifts of God, our community
All of us creation, all of us beloved,
Fiercely and wonderfully made.

Lyrics: Megan Rohrer, Susan Strouse and Judith Dancer

We Walk in Sight of All the World

This hymn, set to the tune of We Walk by Faith and Not by Sight, can also be sung to the tune of Balm in Gilead, Where Charity and Love Prevail and The King Shall Come. Written to advance the idea that we are one with all creation and our perceptions are reciprocal to the perception of creation. If I touch a tree, then I am also touched by the tree.

We walk in sight of all the world;
Are seen by all that see:
The moon the lake, the tree, the cloud,
And by the Mystery

We sense the earth beneath our feet;
We stand on holy ground.
The earth delights to bear our weight,
And hear our footsteps sound.

We hear the singing of the birds,
And answer in return;
Are joined by all that hum and call,
Each other's song to learn.

We see the height and majesty
Of mountain peaks afar;
Our bones cry out to rock and stone,
"We are of the same star!"

O all unfolding Mystery,
O Source and Fire true!
In our becoming one with all,
May we be one with you!

Lyrics: Sharon Reinbott

This is a Sacred World

This hymn, set to the tune of This is My Father's World, imagines God as the force behind the Big Bang, whose light you can now see. Our response is to absorb the beauty and sacredness of the world, to let it permeate us and to accept the gift of death by living our soul dream, our truest self, which is deep inside each of us. It firmly states that the same creative force that started it all has now come to birth in each one of us.

This is a sacred world. The universe divine
Pours into night creative might, and we reflect its shine.
This is a sacred world. We see its firstborn light
Creating stars, their worlds and ours flared forth in deepest night.

This is a sacred world. It permeates our sense.
The moon, the tree, the cloud, the sea, in pure magnificence.
This is a sacred world. Oh may it all employ
To listen well, with every cell, transformed in wonderous joy.

This is a sacred world, though death will have its due.
It makes me dare to live aware, my deepest dream pursue.
This is a sacred world. May I arise and see
Primeval flame, creation's name, now come to birth in me.

Lyrics: Sharon Reinbott

Arising, Illumining Source all Divine

This hymn, set to the tune of Immortal, Invisible God Only Wise, depicts God as breaking into creation, inspiring creativity in us. Lutheran baptismal liturgy says that we are to bear God's creative and redeeming world into the world. We have a lot to say about redemption; we have very few hymns about our creative being.

Arising, illumining Source all Divine!
O Wave of pure Beauty, a round all you shine.
You burst irrepressibly into the world,
Igniting the spark of a new life unfurled.

To life you awaken and touched by your fire,
To life we awaken in creative desire.
You beckon us onward; you call us to be
A part of the story, the great Mystery!

May we not refuse you, but open to all
The life you infuse as we answer the call,
To stand in the Mystery, chosen to be
Awakened, emboldened, creative and free!

Lyrics: Sharon Reinbott

We Are People Transforming

This hymn challenges us to not turn away from those who are different or differently abled, to bear pain, to allow our hearts to break and to offer these broken hearts to God. In this offering we become transformed and made new.

We are people transforming, seeds in the earth;
We are lifted by God's love, to die to new birth.
We emerge tender shoots, in the Spirit our roots.
We are dying, we are rising and bearing much fruit.

But we turn to our comfort, rules we respect;
And we turn from the mis'ry of those we neglect.
All our turning's in vain, never soothing the strain
Of our hearts now breaking open to all of their pain.

We behold God's beloveds, widen our view,
And our hearts sweetly soften, to love them a new.
Our indifference aside, and with Jesus as Guide,
We incarnate His compassion, with hearts open wide.

Let us join hands together, wait for new birth,
To be lifted in God's own embrace of the earth
Where we offer anew broken hearts that are true:
In our dying and arising, transformed and made new.

Lyrics: Sharon L. Reinbott

Liturgical Hymns

Gathering Songs

Gathering Song to the Tune of Lady Gaga's Paparazzi

We're gathered around, our hymnals are out
Got my stole on it's true, need that icon of you
It's so mystical, we are so religical

Collar and jeans, your cross so glamorous
Not sure what it means, but in this room tonight
We've got water, bread and wine, there's even candlelight
'Cause baby you know that

God's your biggest fan, the bible says God loves me
Papa-son and Spirit
Baby there's no other God above, you know that I'll be your
Faithful clergy

Promise I'll be kind, God became man but stayed devine
Baby you'll be saved, even if you don't feel worthy
Papa-son and Spirit

Lyrics: Megan Rohrer

Call to Worship to the Tune of The Beatles' Blackbird

Welcome to worship this Sunday morn[3]
God is here and the time is right
breathe the breath of life
You were only waiting for this moment to arise.

Welcome to worship this Sunday morn
Breathing as one, together we will sing
Let the church bells ring
You were only waiting for this moment to free.

Prepare your hearts
Prepare your hearts
For the words of God bring change

Lyrics: Megan Rohrer

---

[3] Change these words to match the time of your worship service. The rhyming scheme was originally set to rhyme with worship at night.

Call to Worship to the Tune of Joni Mitchell's Big Yellow Taxi

Welcome to worship, all who shelter in place
Faithful community, full of love and grace

<u>Chorus</u>
God is with you in your home
Even when you feel all alone.
Welcome to worship all who shelter in place.

It's the season of Easter so we celebrate life
With word, bread, wine, water and light
   Chorus

We'll plant seeds of hope as our love grows
So get present, from your head to your toes
   Chorus

Lyrics: Megan Rohrer

Gathering Song to the Tune of Bob Dylan's Times They are a Changin'

Come gather 'round people wherever you roam
And admit all the trials and troubles you've sown
we gather together, but still feel alone

our hearts and our minds are ragin'
we were all dust, till God put breath in our bones
so our lives, they are a chang - in'

Come prophets and skeptics and all who dream dreams
the last will be first and the bound shall be free
through bread, wine and water, what's promised shall be
We all equally need savin'
Christ died on the cross for you and for me
so our lives, they are a-changin'

Come listen to the Gospel please heed the call
It's promise is truth and pardon for all
We must take that message outside of these walls
To counter all the hatin'
Let's sing so loud, they hear us in the hall
Because our lives, they are a-changin'

Lyrics: Megan Rohrer

Gospel Acclamations

Gospel Acclamation to the tune of Lady Gaga's Poker Face

<u>Chorus</u>
Ha-lle-lu-jah, hallelujah Praise be to Christ, hear these holy words
Ha-lle-lu-jah, hallelujah Praise be to Christ, hear these holy words

Please read my, please read my
Deacon read the Gospel of the day
(this week it comes from Matthew[4])

Please read my, please read my
Deacon read the Gospel of the day
(this week it comes from Matthew)

ga-ga Gospel of the day, gospel of the day
ga-ga Gospel of the day, gospel of the day

The Gospel is read and the chorus is repeated.

Lyrics: Megan Rohrer

---

[4] Change the name of the book as is appropriate for the reading.

Gospel Acclamation to the tune of The Beatles' Yellow Submarine

<u>Chorus</u>
Hallelujah and praise be to Christ
Praise be to Christ, praise be to Christ
Hallelujah and praise be to Christ
Praise be to Christ, praise be to Christ

The Gospel of the day is read and the chorus is repeated.

Lyrics: Megan Rohrer

Gospel Acclamation to the tune of Joni Mitchell's Twisted

Alleluia   God to whom shall we go?
Alleluia   God to whom shall we go?
You have the words to eternal life
 Allelu---------ia

Lyrics: Megan Rohrer

Prayers of the People

Prayers of the People to the Tune of The Beatles' Across the Universe

Let prayers raise like incense through the church while we repent
Spread forgiveness, unbind made-up-minds and wallets
across the universe
Bless our leaders, of all kinds, bishops, pastors, civic minds
Families, pets, all humankind across the universe

<u>Chorus</u>
And so we pray together   Oh
God is gonna change the world
I am gonna change the world
You are gonna change the world
We are gonna change the world

We pray for those who are pain, and those who bring back health again
Prayers to end poverty and war across the universe
End destruction waste and greed, so we can help out those in need
Restore peace and prosperity across the universe
Chorus

Protect all children, save the earth help us understand the true worth
Of all who live and breathe across the universe
Help us remember we are loved by the holy trinity above
Who calls us to be stewards of, all the universe
Chorus

Lyrics: Megan Rohrer

Prayers of the People to the Tune of Lady Gaga's Bad Romance

<u>Chorus</u>
Ohhh ohh ohhh, ohhhh ohhhhh, let us do all in love
Ohhh ohh ohhh, ohhhh ohhhhh, let us do all in love
Ubi caritas, est cor nostrum, omnia nos amore,[5] let us do all in love

We pray for the hungry, we pray for disease
We pray for outcasts and for all to be free
May you feel loved, love, love, love, we want God's love

We pray for the lonely and for the depressed
We pray for all workers and those who are stressed
May you feel loved, love, love, love, we want God's love

<u>Bridge</u>
Live and love the best you can, you and me were gonna live forgiven
Live and love the best you can, you and me were gonna live forgiven
Chorus

We pray for children and for their parents
We pray for teachers and all who pay rent
May you feel loved, love love love
We want God's love

We pray for the war torn and those who bring peace
for politicians and the whole diocese
May you feel loved, love love love
We want God's love
Bridge
Chorus

Lyrics: Megan Rohrer

---

[5] Latin translation: where there is charity, there is our heart, we do all things with love

Prayers of the People to the Tune of Bob Dylan's To Make You Feel My Love

When the rain is blowing in your face
And the whole world is on your case
All you need is a little grace
To help you feel God's love.

For all the hungry, and the black and blue
All who live on sidewalks and avenues
When it feels like there is nothing we can do
May you feel God's love.

When death and illness turns life to gray
and there's nothing left to do but pray
We'll come together and always say
May you feel God's love

<u>Bridge</u>
When you think no there's no love left for me
Or you can only think of life's regret
The winds of change are blowing wild and free.
There's even more forgiveness for you yet

When the rain is blowing in your face
And the whole world is on your case
All you need is a little grace
To help you feel God's love.

Lyrics: Megan Rohrer

Prayers of the People to the Tune of Joni Mitchell's Clouds

Hear O God our humble prayer
May it rise like incense in the air
Spread Your forgiveness everywhere
Heal us with Your grace
May your will on Earth be done
Bring equal rights to everyone
Erase the pain from what we've left undone
Help us follow Your way

Chorus
Surely God is with us now
As love abounds in our shelter-house
Hear our prayers, answer our call
Shower us with mercy, great All in All

Strengthen leaders of all kinds
Bishops, pastors, all civic minds
Make war and conflict hard to find
And give us bread each day
Care for all creatures high and low
Our love for our neighbors grow
May Your blessings overflow
Help us follow Your way
Chorus

Lift us up when we're feeling down
May wealth and our health abound
Protect the helpers all around
Fill them with Your grace
Keep safe all children who were born
Repair the families that feel torn
Blessings for all who mourn
Take the sting out of the grave
Chorus

Lyrics Megan Rohrer

Prayers of the People to the Tune of Stay with Me by Sam Smith

<u>Chorus</u>
Won't you pray with me?
For love and equality
This world needs peace
So darling, pray with me

After each set of prayers repeat the chorus.

Lyrics Megan Rohrer

Prayers of the People to the Tune of the Eurythmics' Sweet Dreams (Are Made of These)

We pray for the leaders of our faith,
And all who are stewards of this place
For their time and talents we say thanks
Because everybody needs prayers for something

Verse 2
Some of them want to do healings
Some of them want to be healed by you
Some of them want to love you
Some of them want to be loved by you

Chorus
Our prayers like incense, raise to God
Our hearts and intentions, raise to God
Worries and sorrows, raise to God
False impressions, raise to God
Our thanksgivings, raise to God

We pray for those in need of peace,
And all who struggle with disease
Or from addiction need release
Because everybody needs prayers for something
Verse 2
Chorus

We pray for our minds, hearts and health,
Help us to learn to love our selves
Free us from debt and share our wealth
Because everybody needs prayers for something
Verse 2
Chorus

Lyrics Megan Rohrer

Passing the Peace

Passing of the Peace to the Tune of The Beatles' I Wanna Hold Your Hand

Oh please, say to me -
We are all kin in Christ
And please, say to me -
I wanna shake your hand
I wanna shake your hand.
I wanna shake your hand.

The peace, of Christ is with you
And also with you,
So please, get off your seat
Share a sign of God's peace
Share a sign of God's peace.
Share a sign of God's peace.

And when you greet me I feel happy, inside
It's such a blessing my dear God
I won't hide, I won't hide

The peace, of Christ is with you
And also with you,
So please, get off your seat
And share a sign of God's peace
Share a sign of God's peace.
Share a sign of God's peace.

And when I greet you I feel Spirit, inside
It's such a blessing that I must
Spread your light, spread your light

Repeat verse 1

Lyrics Megan Rohrer

Passing of the Peace to the Tune of Joni Mitchell's The River

The peace of Christ is with you, and also with you
Share that peace with others in the chat box too
Feel God's peace I pray
There is love here, bursting through your screen
Enough blessings to make it through this crazy scene
I send you God's peace today

Yes I send you Christ peace from far away
Enough peace to make it through the whole day
Oh receive Christ peace I pray
As we shelter in place

The peace of Christ is with you, and also with you
Share that peace with others in the chat box too
Feel God's peace I pray

Lyrics Megan Rohrer

Offering

Offering Song to the tune of Adelle's Rolling in the Deep

There's a fire that's burning in a bush
Calling you out and giving you a push
Sex workers will go to heaven before you
Don't put stock in the good works that you do

There's no safety in wealth or property
Waste and neglect are another form of greed
There's a fire that's burning in a bush
Calling you out and giving you a push

Bridge
Give all you have to those in need
And we'll become equal in our vulnerability
Give all you have to those in need
And in your want you'll find we already have it

Chorus
All in All
And it was always free
From the font to the empty tomb
Grace is never, never cheap

Baby I have a story to be told
About six gold coins and a careless widow
As she searches for the one that's on the loose
So shall God always long for you
Bridge
Chorus

Seek and find all your treasured gold
Invest it wise that's where your heart will go
Count your blessings and honor what you owe
Pay me back in time, you'll reap just what you sow
Bridge
Chorus

Lyrics Megan Rohrer

Communion

Communion to the Tune of The Beatles' Hey Jude

<u>Chorus</u>
Na na na na-na na na, na-na na na, Je- sus (repeat)

Je-sus, he took the bread
Gave thanks and said: Take and eat
This is my body, I'm giving to you
Yes this is true, bead of heaven

Je-sus, he blessed the cup
his blood creates for us holy kinship
so we remember God's promises to us all
despite the fall, we are all God's children

<u>Bridge</u>
And every time you drink this cup
Think of Christ and remember
All your sins are forgiven
Chorus

Holy one, hosannas to you
Blessed are all who come to your table
we remember the Saints from other times
In this bread and wine, pour out your Spirit

Creator God, who lives among us
we lift your name, above all others
and we remember your sacrifice for our sins
let your reign begin and continue forever, and ever and ever

Silence for the breaking of the bread, followed by the chorus repeated as long as communion or fading out.

Lyrics Megan Rohrer

Communion to the Tune of Jodi Mitchell's All I Want

After supper Jesus took the bread
Broke it, gave thanks and gave it to all eat
He said, please eat some, please eat some, it's my body
Eat it in remembrance of me

Blessed be God, the highest God
Creator of heaven, stars and the sea
God called forth the light and raised mountains to their height
Called Moses and the Israelites out of slavery
Do you want, do you want, do you want to taste salvation?

Then he took the wine, gave thanks and said
This is the cup is a new covenant
He said, please drink some, please drink some, it's my blood
Drink this in remembrance of me

May your kingdom come, on earth as in heaven
Give us each our daily bread
Forgive our debts as I forgive those who have debts with me
For yours is the power and the glory
Do you want, do you want, do you want to taste salvation?

Breathe your spirit on this bread and wine
Renewing and sustaining all who receive
Pour your spirit, pour your spirit on all who gather together
Knit together with love all of humanity

Lyrics Megan Rohrer

Communion to the Tune of Lady Gaga's Telephone

Raise your hearts and minds to God who's above all
with the saints, and prophets have followed the call

Holy, holy, holy, we lift our voice to you
Blessed be your name, keep us forever true

On the night he was betrayed, Christ took the bread
Broke it, gave thanks, and give it for all to eat

Then after supper, he took the cup and gave thanks
Gave it for all to drink, said this is my blood, eh

The cup of the new covenant, I've shed for all of you
Each time you eat or drink this meal, think of me too

<u>Chorus</u>
Our God in heaven, hallow'd be your name
Your kingdom come, will be done, on earth as in heaven
Save me from temptation and keep me from all sin
all power and glory is yours again and again

<u>Bridge</u>
A, A, A, A, A, A, A, A, A, A, A, men
(Christ Body!) A, A, A, A, A, A, A, A, A, A, A, men
(And Blood!) A, A, A, A, A, A, A, A, A, A, men
(Now were one body!) A, A, A, A, A, A, A, A, A, A, A, men

Come now Holy Spirit and put your blessings here
Gather us into one and take away our fear

The bread is broken.

[chanted twice]
Sin all you want, but believe even more,
love your neighbor and help the poor
Out in the streets, or in the store,
God loves you forever more

Lyrics Megan Rohrer

Communion to the tune of The House of the Rising Sun

The peace of Christ be with you all
And also with you
Lift your hearts, breathe the breath of life
O God, we sing to you

It's right, and good and we know we should
Give thanks and praise to God
Who made the earth, the sea and stars
And declares that we are good

This song we sing, is an echoing
From our ancestors of faith
Holy, holy holy are you
And Blessed be your name

On the night in which he was betrayed
Jesus took the bread
Gave thanks and gave it to all to eat
A taste of the feast to come

After supper, he took the cup
A new covenant in blood (he said)
Each time you drink, remember me,
And pray as I was taught:

God in heaven, we raise your name
And work towards your kingdom now
May we follow you, with hearts that are true
Protect us all our days

These are the gifts of God for all
God, put your Spirit here
And on all who've gathered for this in this space
May we eat and drink our fill

Lyrics: Megan Rohrer

Communion to the Tune of Cups as Performed by Anna Kendrick

Jesus had a ticket for the long way 'round
A few disciples for the way
They shared Shabbat and some sweet company
And said, "I'm leaving tomorrow, wha-do-ya say?"

Chorus
When I'm gone, when I'm gone
You're gonna miss me when I'm gone
You're gonna miss me by my hair
You're gonna miss me everywhere, oh
You're gonna miss me when I'm gone

During supper he took the bread
Broke it and gave it to all to eat
It's my body, it's broken for all of you
So eat it and think of me
Chorus

After supper he took the cup
And gave it for all to drink
It's my blood and forgiveness for all your sins
Drink it and remember to think
Chorus

My sins are gone, my sins are gone
I can't believe my sins are gone
You can tell by the way I walk
You can tell by the way I talk, oh
Yes, my sins are really gone!

Lyrics Megan Rohrer

Sending Songs

Go in Peace to the Tune of The Beatles' Let it Be

May God's face shine upon you.   And clear a path before your feet
Praying for tomorrow, Go in peace
Blessed and forgiven,   Children of God you'll always be
Claim your wholeness, Go in peace

Chorus:
Go in peace, go in peace, go in peace, go in peace
in service, love and wisdom   Go in peace

And when the bay is foggy.   And suffering is all we see
May joy replace our sorrows, Go in peace
May we be light in darkness.   For the whole world's in need.
Help us bring justice, Go in peace
Chorus

Lyrics Megan Rohrer

Sending to the Tune of Lady Gaga's Just Dance

This is the end of our worship (oh oh oh, oh)
And soon we will all start to rush, start to rush babe
Going to a club or to your home (home, home, home)
Where are my keys, don't forget your phone, phone

Bridge
But, before you head out the door
Remember that God loves you and won't keep score
So go love your neighbor and serve the poor
You are blessed by Christ forever more

Chorus
Go in peace, be safe   da doo doo doo
Go in peace, don't forget to pray   da doo doo doo
Go in peace, come back next Sunday   duh duh duh duh
peace, peace, peace, go in peace

Lyrics Megan Rohrer   :

Sending to the Tune of Joni Mitchell's Circle Game

May Christ dwell in your heart like morning dew
And may your roots be grounded in love
Have confidence, God's wisdom is inside
Filled with the Spirit from above

Lift your head up   off the ground
And you'll find God's   all around
Creation's a kaleidoscope of grace
No matter where you're going
No matter where you've been
The lost shall all be found
By God's love again

May the breath of God refill you
Beyond length, height, and depth
May your goals exceed what seems true
And be followed by peaceful rest

May the roads rise up to meet you
May the winds always be at your back
May God be found in all you say and do
May you never be judged for what you lack

Lyrics Megan Rohrer

Go My Children, With My Blessing

Go my children, live forgiven, fabulous and free
Walking proud or in isolation, always with me
Here we share a sacred story, full of tragedy and glory
Go my children, live forgiven, fabulous and free

Go my children, claim your future, all you long to be
Learn to love and love by living your full diversity
Here we learn to love our neighbor,
                    pass the peace and feed the stranger
Go my children, claim your future, all you long to be

Lyrics Megan Rohrer

God Be with You Through Transition

A hymn for celebrating trans individuals, to the tune of God Be With You Till We Meet Again.

God be with you till we meet again
Your naming help redefine you
Preferred gender prounouns always find you
God be with you till we meet again

Refrain:
Till we meet, till we meet
Your next stage of transition complete
Till we meet, till we meet
God be with you till we meet again

God be with you till we meet again
Hormone treatments realign you
Endrocrinologyist to guide you
God be with you till we meet again
Refrain

God be with you till we meet again
May your health and shape satisfy you
Full of self esteem inside you
God be with you till we meet again
Refrain

Lyrics: Megan Rohrer

Blessing and Dismissal

To the Tune of Rude by Magic!

Blessings are offered and those gathered respond with the following refrain:

Chorus:

Why you gotta be so rude? I'm a saint and a sinner too
Why you gotta be so rude? God blesses us anyway
Blesses us anyway
Go in peace (yeah, no matter what they say)
Go in peace (and we'll be your family)
Why you gotta be so rude

Lyrics Megan Rohrer

Go in Peace to the Tune of A-Ha's Take on Me

Chorus
Go in   peace (go in peace)
Go in   peace (go in peace)
Christ is Ris'n
Hallelujah

Lyrics Megan Rohrer

About the Authors

Judith Lavender Dancer, Choreographer of the Soul, Registered Somatic Movement Therapist, Dancer and Collage Artist, has been dancing and moving her entire life as she connects with Spirit through movement. She was baptized in 2005 as a Lutheran and participated in a Lakota pipe ceremony community for 2 years before that. Very connected to the Divine Feminine, it is the basis for her work, community, and ceremony; her personal daily practice includes embodied meditation in the tradition of Dharma Ocean.

Orion was born in Lancaster, Pennsylvania, on All Saints' Day, 1950 and he died in January of 2018 in San Francisco. After receiving his Bachelor of Arts degree in Music Education from Lenoir-Rhyne University, Hickory, NC, he served in the United States Navy for three years. Following his honorable discharge from the Navy at Pearl Harbor, he continued his education at Rutgers University, completing the Master of Fine Arts Degree in Theater Arts. He did additional graduate work at the University of Hawaii and Westminster Choir College.

During his long and distinguished career, he was a Professor of Theater Arts at Newberry College, Newberry, SC, where he was Chair of the Department of Theater and Director of the College Players.

Upon moving to San Francisco, he served as Director of Music for First United Lutheran Church in San Francisco. It is here where he found an outlet for his musical talent in playing piano, pipe organ and electronic keyboards. He considered himself a "spiritual traveler" and endeared himself to a plethora of people from many faith backgrounds and cultures.

He left this note among his possessions: "When I die": ORION: Musician, Actor, Seeker

The Rev. Dr. Susan M. Strouse is a native of Pottstown, PA (near Philadelphia) and is a graduate of Antioch University/Philadelphia and the Lutheran Theological Seminary in Gettysburg. She has served congregations in Buffalo, NY and Novato, CA. Most recently she served First United, Lutheran Church, San Francisco from 2004 - 2017. In 2005 she received a Doctor of Ministry degree from the Pacific School of Religion in Berkeley. Her area of study and interest is *inter*faith and *intra*faith theology, particularly working with congregations and clergy to explore the meaning of being a Christian in our religiously diverse world. In 2016 she published her book, *The INTRAfaith Conversation: How Do Christians Talk Among Ourselves about INTERfaith Matters?* She has been a presenter at the North American Interfaith Network conference and the Parliament of the World Religions in 2015 and 2018. Pastor Susan resides in Berkeley, CA.

Sharon Reinbott's earliest church memory was watching her father's finger point to the words of the hymn everyone was singing. Too young to read, she could only guess the connection between the singing and the printed page, but the singing was her favorite part of the Methodist service. Later, as a young girl, Sharon spent hours in the family basement playing on a little keyboard, and singing and learning hymns from old hymnals, the only source of music in her house. Their images of God became hers.

College, the Sixties, and physics class changed all that. She stopped believing that her short time on the planet was a proving ground for eternity in heaven or hell, as she had been taught. At age 25, she wandered into a Lutheran church and heard about the free grace of God, for all. This was good news! She became a Lutheran, with a fresh understanding of the hymns she sang.

Her Lutheran theology carried her through difficult relationships, through parenting her two sons, and through a career as a software developer. As she neared retirement, she began to study the deep creativity of the cosmos, and the sacredness and consciousness of the evolutionary process. Every atom of her body had been manufactured in the explosion of a star! Perhaps God was not an entity external to the universe, but permeated every particle of it. Wasn't this what incarnation was all about?

She began to search for a life purpose, to find her own vision and essence. After retiring, she fasted in solitude for four days in Death Valley, CA, with the intent of daring to manifest her gifts. On the final day of her fast, she received the message, "Re-envision Christianity. So many people are hurting," and began to write new words for old hymns.

Sharon's work is inspired by many teachers, including Thomas Berry, Pierre Teilhard de Chardin, Sally MacFague, Richard Rohr, and Bill Plotkin. She holds an M.A. degree from Holy Names University in Culture and Spirituality, and lives in Oakland, CA with her partner David.

**The Rev. Dr. Megan Rohrer**, the first openly transgender pastor ordained in the Lutheran church, received a Master of Divinity and Doctor of Ministry and distinguished alumni award from The Pacific School of Religion in Berkeley, CA. The pastor of Grace Lutheran in San Francisco and a chaplain for the San Francisco Police Department, Megan is known for their innovative projects addressing homelessness and poverty and for advocacy on LGBTQ issues.

The recipient of numerous awards in history, music and community service, Megan received an honorable mention as an Unsung Hero of Compassion by Wisdom in Action, with His Holiness the Dali Lama, was named honorary royalty by a traditional Hindu king in Bali, Indonesia, received an honorary doctorate from Palo Alto University and was featured both in Wittenberg, Germany for the 500th Celebration of the Reformation and in Cosmopolitan Magazine.

Megan is the author of 25 books, including a series of progressive, faithful children's books and non-fiction books on LGBTQ issues. *Letters for My Brothers,* which was co-edited with Zander Keig, was a finalist for the Lambda Literary award.

www.ingramcontent.com/pod-product-compliance
Lightning Source LLC
Chambersburg PA
CBHW020959090426
42736CB00010B/1390